Hop on Santa's sleigh and tour The Capital of the U.S.A.

Santa's Visit to Washington D.C.

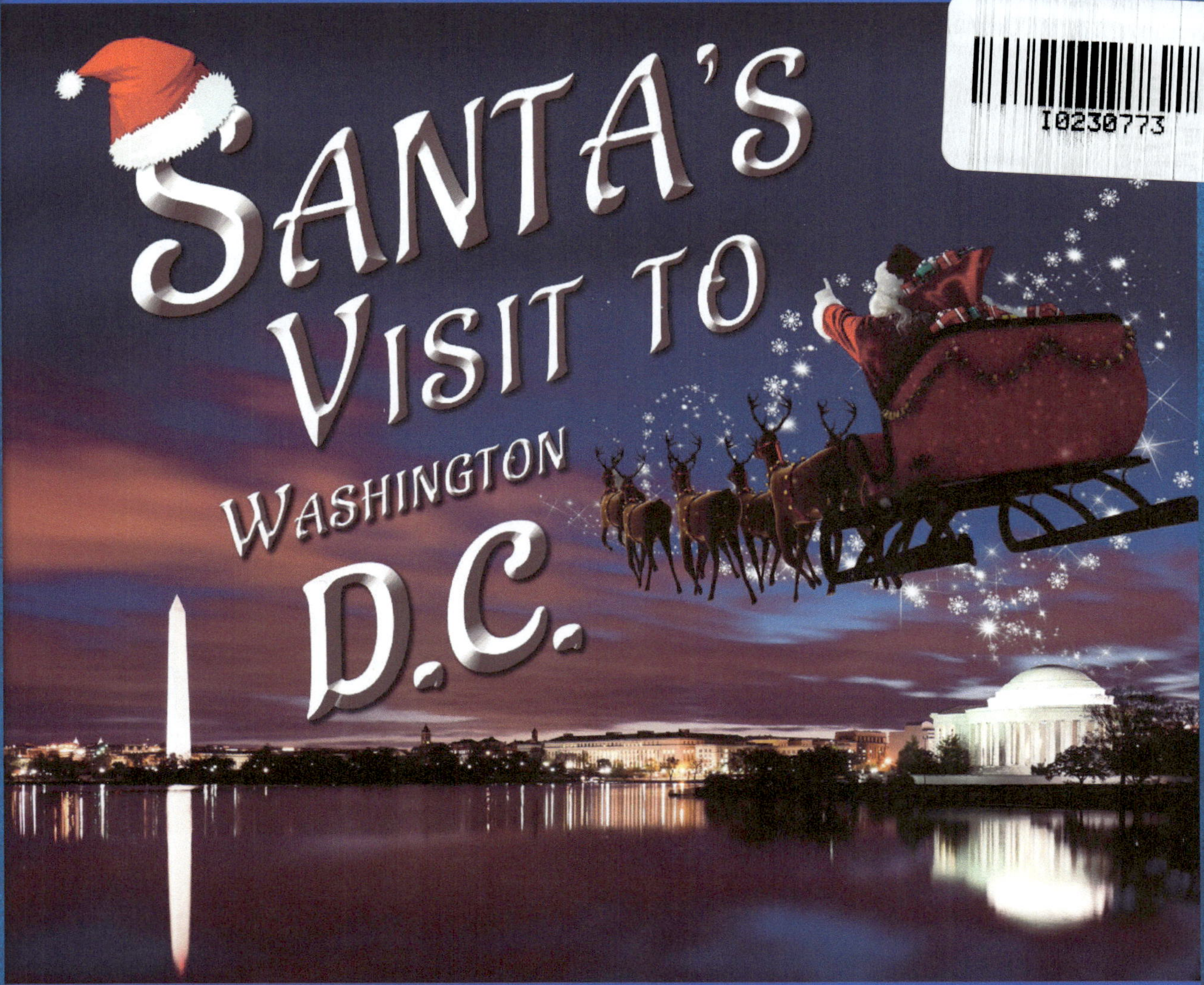

Lynn Roxy Gambrill

Photos by Nick Malambri and Others

Santa's Visit to Washington, D.C.

© Copyright 2024

No portion of this book may be reproduced, stored in a retrieval system or transmitted in any form or by any means—electronic, mechanical, photocopy, recording, scanning, or other—except for brief quotations and critical reviews or articles, without the prior written permission of the author, artist or publisher.

ISBN: 978-1-956581-37-9

Canyon Lake, Texas
www.ErinGoBraghPublishing.com

Cover image designed by Kathleen's Graphics

Washington, D.C. Flag

It's Christmastime in Washington, there's one thing I detect,
Santa needed help this year, to have his list rechecked.

He requested the Supreme Court help him check it twice.
Were Republicans and Democrats naughty? ... Or nice?

So with bags of toys and coal, He loaded up his sleigh.
With Mrs. Claus and the Elves, gifts were on their way!

Though as he entered airspace, he really should have known,
Even HE could not get clearance, for DC's no-fly zone.

To the left and to the right, he cruised so merrily,
Spreading good cheer with his sleigh full of charity.

Military Women's Memorial

His smile was so happy, his heart so content.
As he cruised passed the Washington Monument.

The Pentagon's surveillance caught a red blinking light,
Sleigh bells on radar showed them Rudolph led the flight.

Faster than The President's Race at a Nationals home game,
He whistled and shouted and called them by name;

On George, on Tom, on Abe and Teddy,
They ran to the White House with a pace that was steady.

Then decorated trees, lit up on "The Mall"
For all the States and Territories – 58 in all.

From the Kennedy Center, they all heard music play.
Duke Ellington's jazz and soulful Marvin Gaye.

To John Phillip Sousa, the Elves marched with glee.
It was a heavenly Christmas Symphony.

Near the Jefferson, Elves had a snowball fight,
Since the pink Cherry Blossoms had turned snowy white.

They made snow angels and then built a snowman,
In the District of Columbia's winter wonderland.

The famous team rode their sled to the National Zoo.
Mrs. Claus gave panda bears* clumps of fresh bamboo.

There were elephants and donkeys....and "RINOs" too,
All decked out in their red, white and blue.

Confused on Dupont Circle, Santa flew the wrong way.
Cars circling around, headed straight towards his sleigh!

He pulled on the reins and cleared the traffic below.
His Santa GPS slid down into the snow.

He stopped and pulled over, then parked his sleigh.
Before he knew it, it was towed away!

Held up at the station, by the FBI
They demanded to know where he was going and why.

"I'm just trying to cross the Potomac River.
You can see I've got loads of toys to deliver."

He ended up at the Botanical Garden
Requesting a hasty Presidential pardon.

With still more magic up his sleeve, they hopped back on his sleigh,
Santa said, "Now it's time we all get on our way."

But Mrs. Claus suggested, "Before we go home again,
Let's go to Ford's Theatre...

...and then The Smithsonian."

Not finding a chimney on top of the museum,
Santa snuck in the back hoping no one would see 'em.

From Natural History to Air and Space,
He secretly left presents, all without a trace.

They saw historic monuments, the wall and the pool,

It all felt like a miracle, just like Christmas Yule.

Soaring overhead, Santa saw a Bald Eagle.
"One last place to go, the National Cathedral."

Respectfully pausing his tour 'round the earth,
He knelt to give honor for our Savior's birth.

God sent his son Jesus and that's the real reason,
We joyfully celebrate this holiday season.

And I heard him exclaim as he gave a big wave,

"Ho, Ho, Ho, Merry Christmas!

From the Land of the Free and the Home of the Brave!"

I pledge allegiance to the flag of the United States of America, and to the Republic for which it stands, One Nation, Under God, Indivisible, with Liberty and Justice for all!

With hopes you'll consider the Santa's Visit Collection of Books an annual family Christmas tradition.

Lynn Roxy Gambrill

toured as a featured performer on cruise ships throughout the U.S. and Europe and played for over 20 years as the principal pianist with the 35-piece Trinity Symphony Orchestra.

Lynn is a jazz and classical faculty member at the Community Colleges of Baltimore County, and a member of the Maryland Entertainment Hall of Fame.

She attended both Peabody and Shenandoah Conservatories of Music and holds a Music Education degree from Towson University in Baltimore, Maryland.

Lynn "Roxy" fronted the popular classic rock band, "The Fabulous Hubcaps" and covered lead vocals, piano, sax, flute and clog dancing. She continues to perform hundreds of gigs per year.

santasvisit3@gmail.com   www.facebook.com/santasvisit

Other books by Lynn Roxy Gambrill:

Santa's Visit to Maryland

Roxy Piano Lessons Beginner Course

Recipes for Improvisation - Jazz and Blues

Carols by Christmas

For advanced, intermediate and beginner piano lessons,
Lynn has recorded over 200 videos on YouTube:
www.youtube.com/@roxypianolessons

Joe Caliguro

Special thanks to Joe Caliguro who is not only my husband, but also a native Washingtonian. Joe worked in the city for over 25 years at the US Department of Education, where he was the Director of the Ready to Learn Television program.

Some of Joe's favorite Emmy Award Winning shows were:

Sesame Street, Word World, Arthur, Dragon Tales, Between the Lions, and more! If it was a children's show on PBS, Joe was probably involved at every level.

Nick Malambri

A huge thanks to my good friend, Nick Malambri, for his brilliant photographs! His artistry really brings this book to life. I've known Nick and his fine work for a long time, and his photographs were a perfect match for this poem!

Nick is a Yacht Broker in Destin, Florida for Galati Yachts.

www.galatiyachts.com

www.eastpassimages.com

Kathleen Shields

The "Santa's Visit" series would not be possible without the expert help from my publisher, Kathleen Shields. She has been a God-send and we work together like peanut butter and jelly! She's creative, easy to work with, and very professional.

www.Kathleens-Graphics.com

Brian Hall

Can you imagine growing up with a neighbor that became one of Santa's helpers? That's what happened to me!

Brian Hall and I lived a couple of houses away from each other... and now he's the Santa in my book!

Thank you, Brian, for making "Santa's Visit to Washington D.C." come alive!

References

Photography credits: East Pass Images c/o Nick Malambri, Sarah Gambrill Paul, Robert and Shanica Gambrill, Keri McCord, Tamsen DiBlasio

iStock credits: Wave Break Media, Jim Schlett, Diy13, Coast-to-Coast, Get Up Studio, Perry Spring, Jim Schlett, F11 Photo, Marians Year, Wirestock, vichie81.

Pixabay credits: Custom BPS, 5598375, 12019, Trip Savvy

Holiday Tow Truck credit: David Dennis Photos

* Panda Bears departed the National Zoo on November 8, 2023, so as of the time of this writing they weren't actually there. I included them in the story because they were such a treat for my family to see for so many years!

ERIN GO BRAGH
Publishing

Erin Go Bragh Publishing publishes various genres of books for numerous authors. Their portfolio consists of a 1200-page Vietnamese to English Dictionary, Historical fiction, an award-winning children's educational series, multiple adult novels and memoirs, tween adventure stories, poetry as well as Christian Fiction for all ages. Their objective is to promote literacy and education through reading and writing.

www.ErinGoBraghPublishing.com

Canyon Lake, Texas

www.ingramcontent.com/pod-product-compliance
Lightning Source LLC
Chambersburg PA
CBHW060822090426
42738CB00002B/81